newcontemporaries 99

Selectors
Carolyn Christov-Bakargiev
Susan Hiller
Keith Tyson

Exchange Flags Liverpool
24 September – 7 November 1999
as part of the Liverpool Biennial of
Contemporary Art

South London Collaboration
20 November – 22 December 1999
Beaconsfield
Milch
South London Gallery

with the support of the
Nigel Moores Family Charitable Foundation

Funded by
THE
ARTS
COUNCIL
OF ENGLAND

New Contemporaries 99 will be launched within the broad and ambitious context of the first Liverpool Biennial of Contemporary Art. Our relationship with the city of Liverpool is already established. Moving on from the Tea Factory, where we showed last year, to the extended possibility of comparison with a range of international artists in Trace, not to mention the JM21 painting competition, is a thrilling prospect.

A level of obsession characterizes the work in this show. A lack of flippancy is matched by a serious desire on the artist's part to map the space around them, in relation to time and history. Many seem to draw on elements from different genres to produce close work unconcerned with exterior form.

People often struggle through art school: very obvious career strategies get scrambled. Economic reality bites. The work, this year, feels transient, a practical method to get through and speak by whatever means possible. There is nothing really very funny here, but, on the other hand, this often very physical work is neither literal, dull, nor purposefully engaged with novelty. The gap between such materiality and meaning is apt and subtle. The work is optimistic in that it hints at future possibilities for contemporary art and reaches out with a high level of uncool force and commitment.

I want to thank Carolyn Christov-Bakargiev, Susan Hiller and Keith Tyson for making such an excellent selection. They really concentrated on all the work submitted and throughout the exhausting process worked with discipline and rigour. The discussion that surrounded the work was broad, erudite and general. The catalogue notes deal, however, with individual contributions, in a deliberate recognition of the huge 'jump' between the general and the specific, which characterizes a 'send in' show.

Every year the Board of New Contemporaries considers what form the exhibition should take. Our primary job, though, is to select the selectors, ensure that all the applicants have a proper hearing and deliver an exhibition where all the selected work is allowed a sympathetic space to flourish.

We are, as ever, immensely grateful to the Nigel Moores Family Charitable Foundation for its continuing commitment to New Contemporaries.

Sacha Craddock

24 September – 7 November

Walker House
Exchange Flags
Liverpool L2 3YL

South London Collaboration
20 November – 22 December 1999

Beaconsfield
Newport Street
London SE11 6AY

newcontemporaries 99

Milch
2-10 Tinworth Street
London
SE11 5EH

South London Art Gallery
65 Peckham Road
London SE5

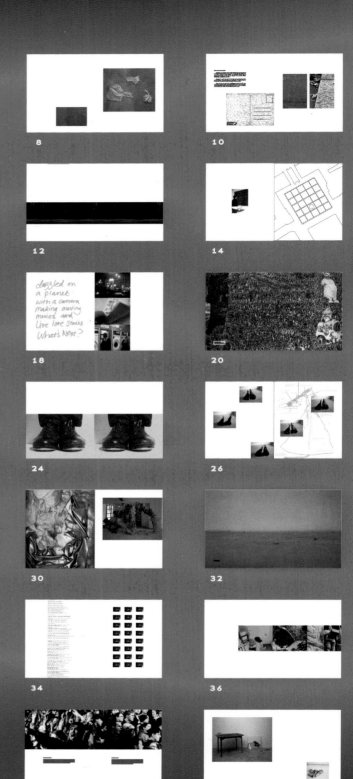

Athanasios Argianas

CLEAR
silicone glue and water

Have you any sins to confess?

Scapegoat is an art project made up of 49 postcards which are being sent out by mail and returned to make up a final image. The title of the piece refers to the goat which, according to Jewish tradition, was symbolically imbued with the iniquities of the people and cast into the wilderness. It is also after William Holman Hunt's painting of the same title.

Scapegoat is a work about guilt and sin, about event and record and about private and public. This project requires your participation. You should confess at least one sin. You will thus be absolved from every sin that you confess.

Please write your sins on the back of the **Scapegoat** postcard, and then return the postcard to the above address. Your postcard, along with the other 48 postcards will be reassembled to make one large image (above). When the piece is displayed only the image will be visible. Your sins will be revealed to no-one.

SCAPEGOAT ¹/₄₉
(49 Postcards)
Charlie Birch, 1999.

David Blandy
RING
video projection

Cleo Broda

INFORMATION STATION 1998

PROPOSAL FOR LIVERPOOL: LOCATION GUIDE (SUBJECT PENDING)

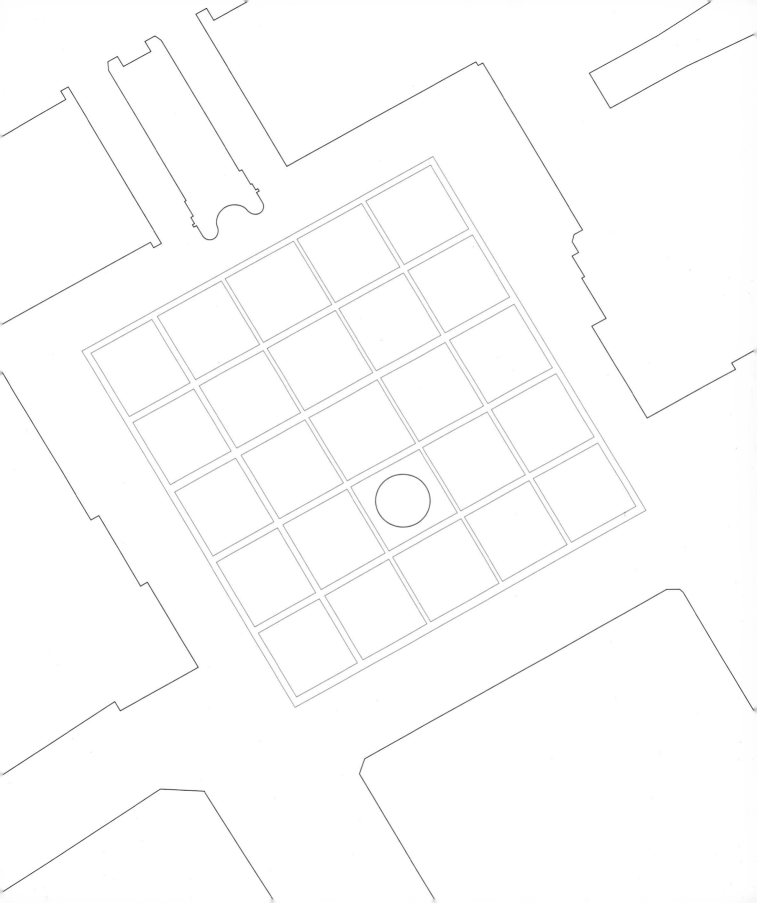

K.R Buxey
LEGION
video projection

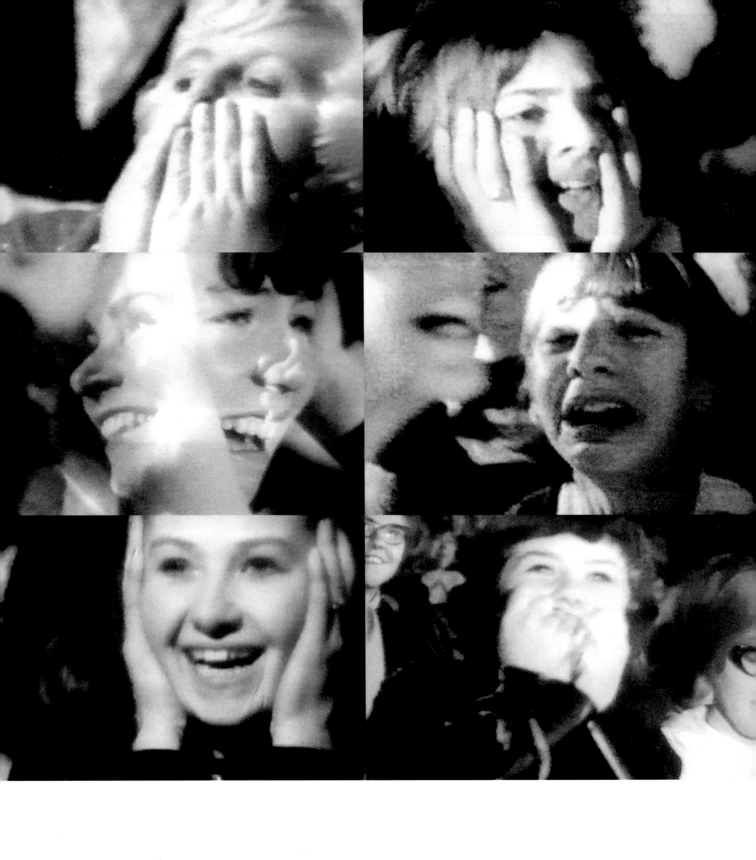

dazzled on
a planet
with a camera
making moving
movies and
live love stories

What's Next?

Louise Camrass
ST VALENTINE'S DAY
stills from film

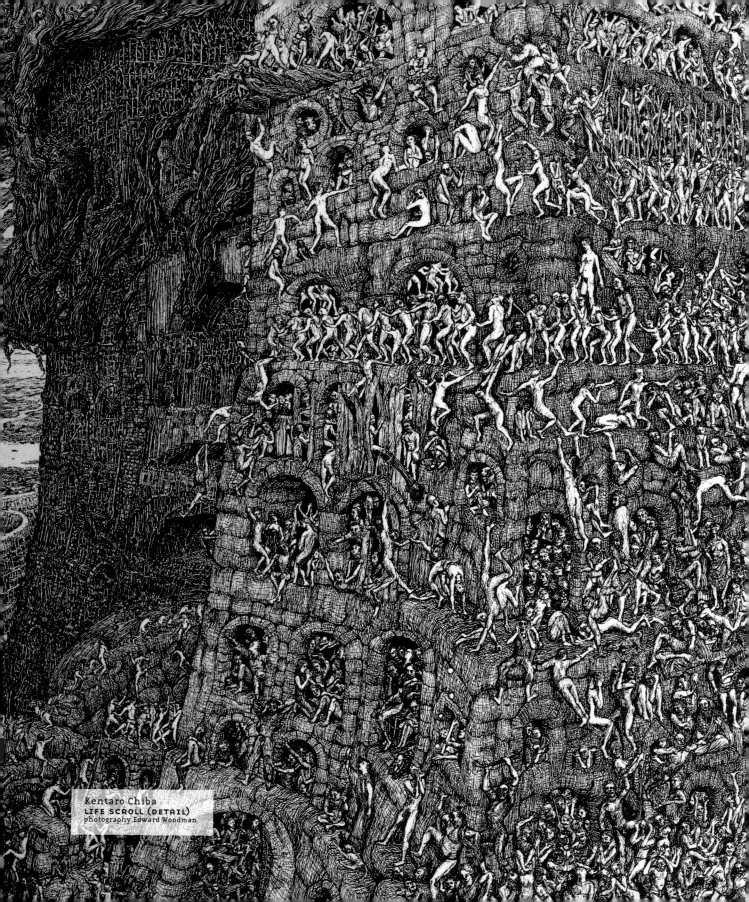

Kentaro Chiba
LIFE SCROLL (DETAIL)
photography Edward Woodman

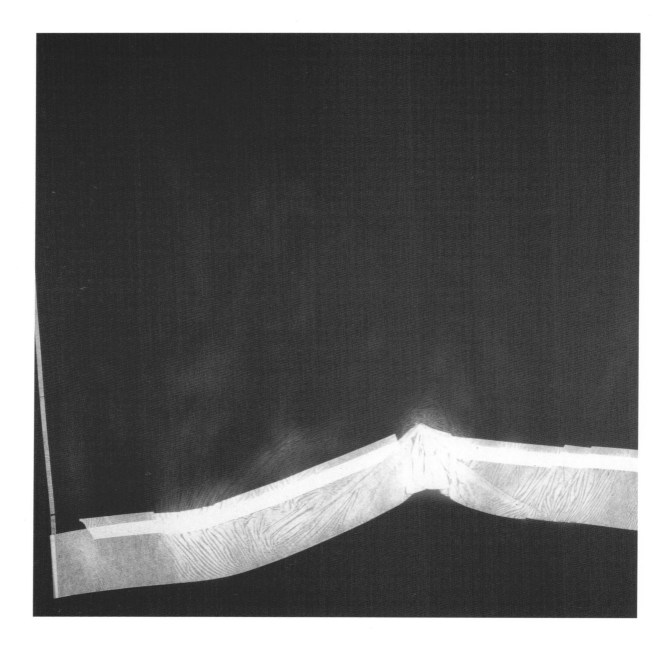

Ben Cook
THE PASSION OF THE RED ARMY
in the collection of Trevor Johnson, VIA Communications
photography Edward Woodman

AERIAL VIEW OF THE HARBOUR, MARSEILLES
in the collection of the Arts Council of England
photography Edward Woodman

Richard Cuerden
THE MECHANICS OF PERFORMANCE
video

Andrew Currie
COMFORT MOVEMENTS
video documentation of sculpture

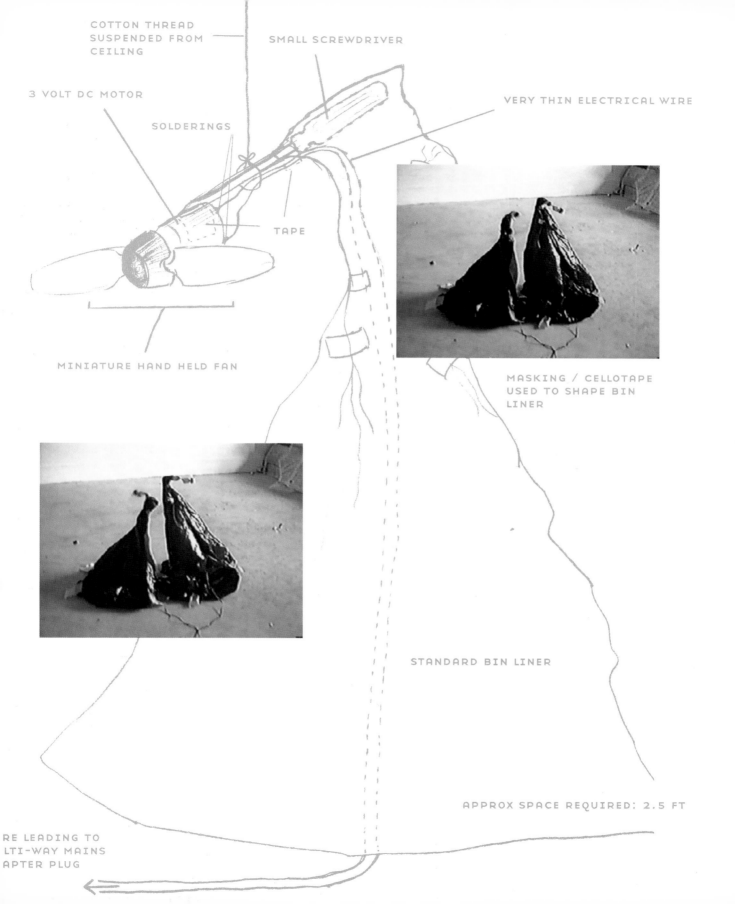

COTTON THREAD
SUSPENDED FROM
CEILING

SMALL SCREWDRIVER

VERY THIN ELECTRICAL WIRE

3 VOLT DC MOTOR

SOLDERINGS

TAPE

MINIATURE HAND HELD FAN

MASKING / CELLOTAPE
USED TO SHAPE BIN
LINER

STANDARD BIN LINER

APPROX SPACE REQUIRED: 2.5 FT

RE LEADING TO
LTI-WAY MAINS
APTER PLUG

Layla Curtis

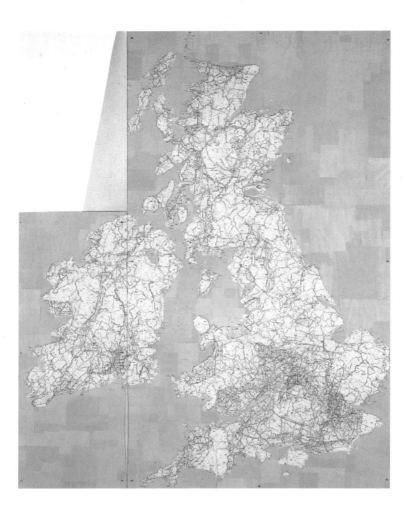

THE UNITED KINGDOM OF JAPAN
collaged road maps
photography Edward Woodman

DETAIL

Jane Fox
SCULPTURE MAY 1999

DETAIL OF MATERIALS
photography Edward Woodman

Clare Gasson
LIPSTICK LINE

The poem must resist the intelligence
Almost successfully. illustration:

A brune figure in winter evening resists
Identity. the thing he carries resists

The most necessitous sense. accept them, then,
As secondary (parts not quite perceived

Of the obvious whole, uncertain particles
Of the certain solid, the primary free from doubt,

Things floating like the first hundred flakes of snow
Out of a storm we must endure all night,

Out of a storm of secondary things),
A horror of thoughts that suddenly are real.

We must endure our thoughts all night,
Until the bright obvious stands motionless in cold.

Man Carrying Thing

the poem must resists the intelliegence almost successfully
the poem must resists the intelliegence almost successfully
illustration

the poem must resists the intelligence almost successfully
illustration
a brune figure in winter night resists evening
a brune figure in winter evening resists identity

a brune figure in evening resists identity
a brune figure in winter evening resists identity

man carrying thing

the poem must resists the intelligence almost successfully
a brune figure in winter evening
a brune figure in winter evening resists identity

illustration
a brune figure in identity
a brune figure in winter evening resists identity
illustration a brune figure in winter evening resists identity

the poem must resists the intelligence almost successfully
illustration
a brune figure in winter evening resiats *** identity

the thing he carries resists the most necessitious sense
the thing he carries resists the most necessitious sense

a brune figure in winter evening resists intelligence
the thing he carries
the thing he carries resists *** the *** most *** necessitious sense
the thing he carries the most necessitous sense

a brune figure in winter evening resists *** identity
the thing he carries resists the most necesstious sense

the poem must resists intelligence almost successfuuly
illustration
a brune figure in winter evening resists identity
the thing he carries resists the most neccessitious sense

a brune figure in winter evening resists identity
the thing he carries resists the most neccessitious sense
accept them, then as secondary
accept them, then as secondary

the thing he carries resists the most neccessitious sense

a brune figure in winter evening resists identity
the thing he carries resists the most neccessitious sense
accept them, then as secondary
parts not quite perceived of the obvious whole
parts not quit perceived of the obvious whole

accept them, then as secondary
parts not perceived
parts not quite perceived of the obvious whole

the thing he carries resists identity
the thing he carries resists the most neccessitious sense
accept them, then as secondary
parts not quite perceived as the obvious whole
parts not quite perceived as the obvious whole

the thing he carries resists *** the *** the neccessitious sense
accept them, then as secondary
parts not quite perceived of the obvious whole

the poem must resists the intelliegence *** almost successfully
illustration:
a brune figure resists *** intelligence
a brune figure in winter evening resists identity
the thing he carries ***
the thing he carries resists the most neccessitious sense
accept them, then
accept them, then as secondary
parts not quite perceived of the obvious whole
uncertain particles of the certain solid

parts not quite perceived of the obvious whole
uncertain particles of the certain solids
the primary free from doubt
accept them, then as secondary
parts not quite perceived *** as the obvious whole
uncertain particles of the solid *** certain solid

the thing he carries resists the most neccesstious sense
the thing he carries resists the most neccessitious sense
accept them, then as secondary
as parts *** parts not quite perceived of the obvious whole
uncertain particles of the certain solid

parts not quite perceived of the obvious whole
uncertain particles of the certain solids

the poem must resists the intelligence almost successfully
illustration:
a brune figure in winter evening resists identity

Jana Haldrich
MAN CARRYING THING
documentation of performance

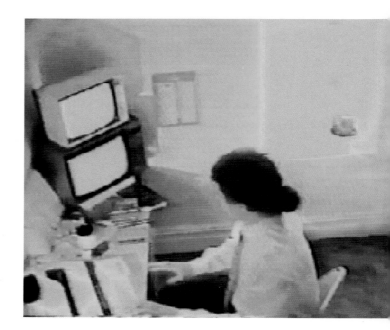

David Harding
VOICES FROM TWO HEMISPHERES
stills from film

We're In Therapy

I miss the first goal, probably as a result of the tea, but I hear and
feel the roar. As I return from the toilet I come down the steps,
above a sea of sky blue and white bobbing up and down deliriously.
"Down with the Villa, you're going down with the Villa". Elation,
aggression, dominance, love and hate in equal measure.

Julie Henry
GOING DOWN
video installation

Free Transfers

I look over their heads towards the Palace supporters away to my
left. They are shouting abuse with distorted and pained faces.
Their initial despair has turned to defiance, temporary defeat to a
thirst for revenge. A small death and the hope of recovery. "You've
only got one song" is not in the same class but it will do until the
players on the pitch supply more ammunition.

Ian Kiaer
VIEW FROM MT. GERIZIM AND MT. EBAL
Sculpture
photography Edward Woodman

THE FIRST CITY
cardboard

Natasha Kidd
PAINTING MACHINE 2
photography Edward Woodman

Nick Laessing

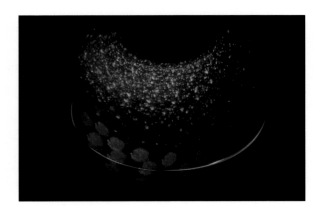

1000RPM TV
video installation

Kenny Macleod
ROBBIE FRASER
video

Hello, my name is Robbie Fraser. Recently I've been doing pretty well. It's great when things go to plan, and you get onto a roll. You know that feeling when after you've invested so much time and effort in a project, and you've persevered through all the distractions and the setbacks and the times when you think you're not getting anywhere, then one day you wake up and things just come together and fall into place so easily. And you say to yourself 'Yes! I've done it, I've really got it together this time'.

It's that feeling that makes it all worthwhile.

Stefanie Marshall
ADOBE DOLLS (DETAIL)
rag, adobe, human hair, straw, banana skins, urine, molasses, pigment
photography Edward Woodman

Tim Meara
STORYVILLE
digital cibachromes

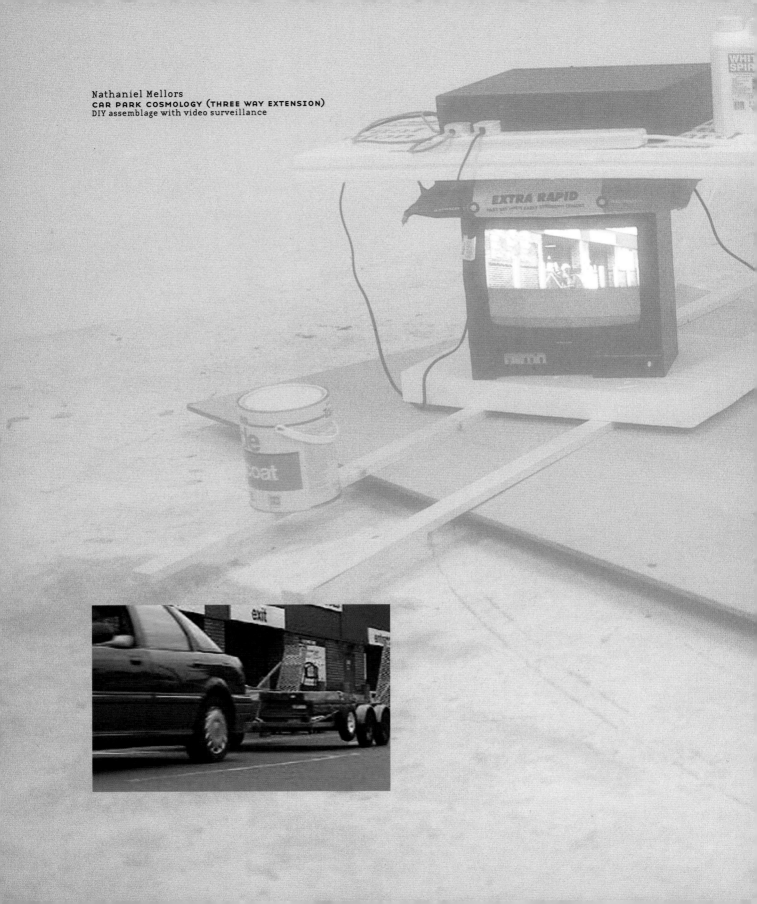

Nathaniel Mellors
CAR PARK COSMOLOGY (THREE WAY EXTENSION)
DIY assemblage with video surveillance

Luke Oxley
ONE THING ON MY MIND
neon sign, books, videos.

Katie Pratt
BURGERHAM 1998
oil on canvas
photography Edward Woodman

WATERGLOO 1998
oil on canvas
photography Edward Woodman

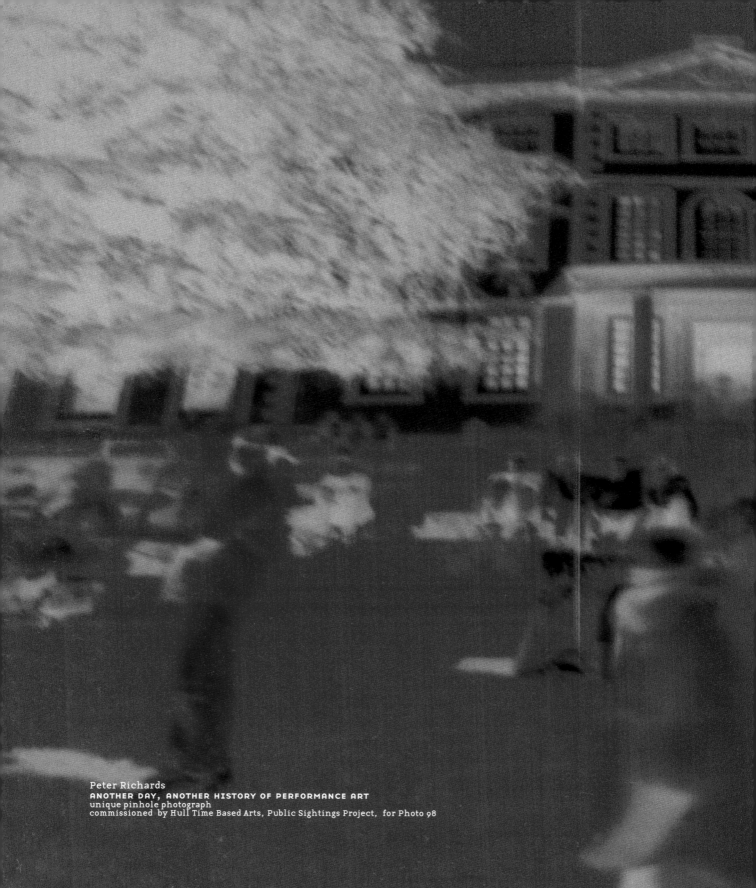

Peter Richards
ANOTHER DAY, ANOTHER HISTORY OF PERFORMANCE ART
unique pinhole photograph
commissioned by Hull Time Based Arts, Public Sightings Project, for Photo 98

32 HOURS

Gaylie Runciman
video

17 HOURS

21 HOURS

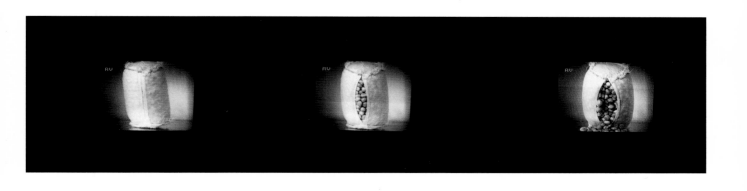

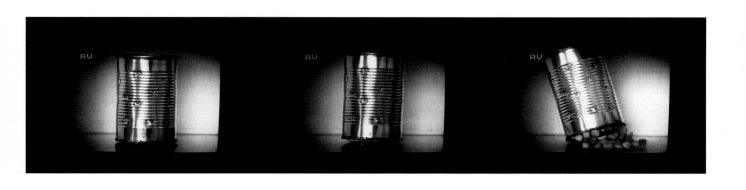

D.J Simpson

CHORD X
alkyd based oil paint on plywood

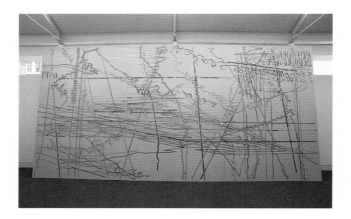

YEAR I (DETAIL)
alkyd based oil paint on plywood
photography Edward Woodman

Louise Spence
MADDLE FARM
photographs

Jayne Stokes
HOME-OLOGY A MOBILE HOME MUSEUM
caravan

Francis Summers
SQUARE HEAD, PALE FACE
video

collection: Liverpool City Museum, May 1941

For Liverpool, I have considered the warehouse in terms of its role in creating the wealth of the city and what this wealth created and what happened to it. The City Museums acquired the collections of the 13th Earl of Derby in 1851 and Joseph Mayer in 1867. From the Shell Guide to England, 1970 'Liverpool became famous for its ivories, gold and jewelry (sic), plant collections, fossils and the Derby collection of birds. The original museum building perished in May 1941, with valuable material'. I would like to research the identity of this lost material. I feel there is an element of these objects being brought together by the destructive experience they were subjected to, as if this extreme event made a single entity out of what was previously separated by taxonomy.

Julian Walker

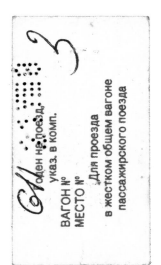

collection, vocabulary, Railway Stations

For London, I can draw on a collection of information which provides the fact that the Russian word for railway station derives from Russian engineers working on the railways around Vauxhall in the 19th century and who took the name back with them. The linguistic link between Vauxhall and Russian railway stations allows me the use of language as a metaphor for movement across space and boundaries.

Nicole Wermers
PALISADES
video projection

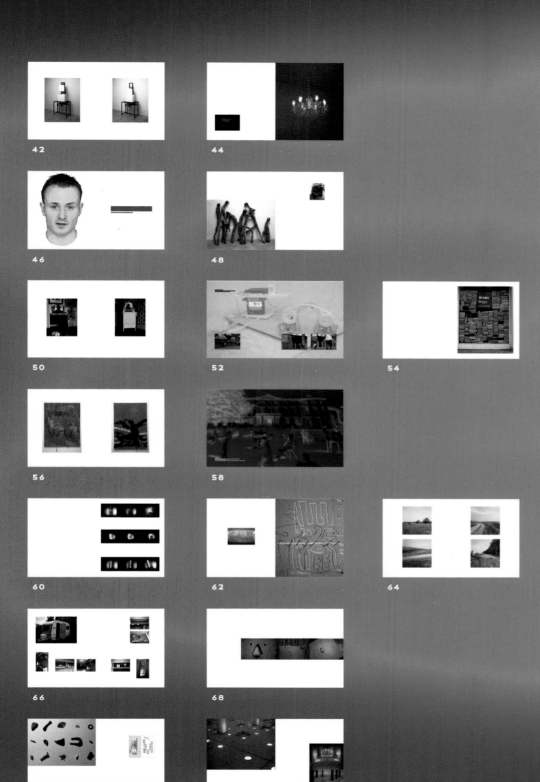

42

44

46

48

50

52

54

56

58

60

62

64

66

68

70

72

These notes on the work of individual artists in this year's New Contemporaries are a result of a series of conversations held at different times between Keith Tyson, Sacha Craddock and Simon Morrissey and between Susan Hiller, Sacha Craddock and Des Lawrence.

At first glance, irreverent, unabashed gestural marks, splodge, drip and ripple their way across the surfaces of Katie Pratt's paintings. Events in paint are then highlighted by a language of small strokes and dashes that act as a forensic study of the initial painting. Like a pseudo-scientific diagram, they highlight the creases and imperfections of paint, translating them into a strange analytical shorthand that is then reclaimed by the ground from which they came.

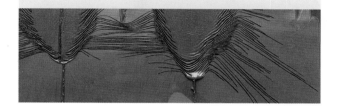

Ben Cook's Found Paintings are reappropriated fabrics originally destined for the manufacture of football shirts. Flawed during their production, the artist selects these mistakes and by stretching them onto a support, the misaligned prints, creases, and failing ink jet traces take on the language of painting. Rejects are salvaged to make works of value.

Using a routing tool D.J Simpson chisels abstract lines at varying degrees, depths and widths into painted plywood boards. An etch-a-sketch doodler meets a DIY enthusiast, in a process of physical excavation. The normal logic of figure and ground in painting is reversed into negative relief. The work, however, doesn't rest on a simple negation of painting, as the physicality of the process and scale asserts itself. It oscillates between making a painting and awkwardly inhabiting physical space, between painting and sculpture, surface and object.

In the United Kingdom work Layla Curtis painstakingly collages the map of Scotland into the boundaries of England, Northern Ireland and Wales. By showing a fictional combination of cities, towns and roads within a familiar form, she automatically questions the very simple presumptions about what comes next and who belongs where. The close observation lends a strange, slow, understanding of a familiar and obvious series of conflicts and questions.

Julian Walker presents small objects meticulously. The unexpected implications of items not normally considered worthy of serious attention are brought to light in his careful, almost obsessional organisation of things. He collects hidden histories and relationships, placing them within the conventional formats of museum display. Each work is a site-specific archaeological investigation, where disturbing or poetic elements are allowed to surface.

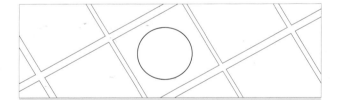

However authorative their form, a diagrammatic account of knowledge will always be partial. In mapping out particular sites, monuments, buildings, Cleo Broda assembles content with a rigorous non-surveying technique. Researching a subject consists of talking to people and stumbling over information which may or may not be useful. The maps are full of opinions, intimate moments, gossip and unsubstantiated history.

Home-ology, A Mobile Home Museum by Jayne Stokes makes a museum of archaeology out of a converted 1970's caravan. Utilising every available space, from the sink to the toilet, she displays banal discarded objects. Fragments are reconstructed in clay with mock archaeological expertise, to show someone a thousand years from now, what might have been. Short explanations on labels attempt to bestow meaning onto that which is normally regarded as meaningless.

Athanasios Argianas creates ephemeral gestures in space. He simulates small incidents. The suggestion of a broken piece of glass on the floor is made with the low tech trompe l'oeil materials of glue and water. Like discarded special effects, they seem to be problems rather than works themselves. The quiet pitch of their abject status makes us question what is, or, what is not worth looking at.

Nicole Wermers Palisades shows an upside down camera ride that gives the impression of somebody walking across the ceiling. This simple change of perspective destabilises our point of view. Lamps or beams in an hotel lobby take on the appearance of sculptures and space is transformed into a landscape of light; an everyday walk through shopping-malls and office spaces is transformed into something quite beautiful and mesmerising.

Territory can't exist without boundary. The boundary can be as simple as the Lipstick Line made by Clare Gasson which defines the boundary itself between space in its simplest sense, the hardcore aesthetics of minimalism and the softer, everyday associations of lipstick. These represent a range of differing conceptual territories.

David Blandy digitally removes the action figures from a violent computer game, leaving the strange echo of the landscape backdrop. He provides us with an unpeopled, natural world. This forest clearing on a panoramic loop surrounds the eye and offers us a host of traditional romantic associations. As a virtual image, however, there is no depth of life here, and the seemingly sublime is a fake.

Natasha Kidd's automatic Painting Machine dips a canvas repeatedly into a vat of white paint, for the duration of the exhibition. As the paint adheres, horizontal lines appear across the surface of the canvas and stalactites of paint form along the bottom edge. Though they are a record of their own mechanical production, each canvas produced will be unique.

Nick Laessing presents two mechanised sculptures. While both are characterised by instability and movement, each creates a unique set of effects and meanings. 1000RPM TV functions only when activated. At a certain moment its television tube, seemingly obsolete, turns from sculptural object into a video spectacle of the planetary cosmos. In the second work a small modern chandelier, domestic and decorous, trembles very slightly, from time to time, hinting at earthquakes and unpredictable disasters.

Richard Cuerden's The Mechanics of Performance uses his own dance skills and personal background as a performer. The simple structure of repeated action, in this video, evokes a world of rigorous discipline and routine, where perfection is the norm. At first aggressive and assertive, an almost hypnotic, trance-like effect is created by the soundtrack of tapping feet. Any expectation of continuity is broken, however, with a jump and lift-off that suspends time and reinforces the break between expectation and result.

Andrew Currie creates a whole world of narrative and dialogue with kinetic sculpture. The use of basic mechanisms and simple movement sets off, in turn, an elaborate play of ritualistic dance and courtly battles. The amorphous creatures made from bin liners act like 3D drawings to perform tableaux which implode, collapse and break down over time.

In Going Down by Julie Henry, the idea is straight forward. The film of the extreme actions and reactions of football supporters watching a match manages to directly convey the intense pitch of ritualistic group dynamic. The camera documents the two sides, the winners and the losers, and at some stage even becomes an object of anger as the crowd vents resentment and elation in equal measure.

In Gaylie Runciman's real-time film of dried peas submerged in water, waiting, whether in real time or in the imagination is crucial. Internal genesis is contained for most of the films by the edge of the glass, tin or muslin; but eventually, and perhaps even in the viewer's absence, the point of explosive action is reached. The matter breaks through or bursts open the container and the process becomes visible.

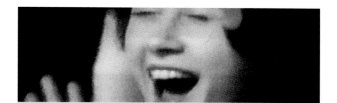

The 1960's girls scream hysterically at the unseen stage in Legion by K.R Buxey. This is another generation, perhaps a parents generation. This archive film footage taken from 1960's pop concerts provides experience of both compulsive behaviour and anthropological observation.

Kentaro Chiba's work is a continuous pursuit, a circle of life and creativity. The Life Scroll is the evidence of a painstaking process, the time spent creating a detailed vision in the full knowledge that this will never be seen in its entirety. This relation between association and image; subconscious quotation, recognition and slowed snails pace, delivered over his lifetime, is an extended multi-angled sense of visual and creative inevitability.

Stefanie Marshall's Adobe Dolls are made quite obsessively; scores of these witchy, scary, smelly totems are already in existence. The repetition is not about reinforcing artistic or aesthetic presence, but is perhaps evidence of a cathartic process for the artist and a means of release.

Jane Fox's work involves a huge element of public risk. The resulting sculptural mass can be highly erratic. Semi-theatrical constructions grow out of the combined force of time, material and pretence. The relationship between weight, lightness and dramatic effect is where the presence temporarily resides.

A tableaux of delicate and small objects, placed specifically and deliberately in relation to each other by Ian Kiaer, creates a poignant context. Somehow the strange combination of spatial arrangement and implied narrative is a reminder of a biblical scene, almost forgotten or only seasonally-glimpsed through images of the nativity.

Nathaniel Mellors' films people leaving the exits of a DIY store with their purchases. At a certain point he makes exactly those purchases and later he arranges this material, in the gallery, to achieve an informal sculptural assemblage. Using the mechanism of an arbitrary system, presumably, frees him to explore aesthetics without the guilt of choice; in a constant search to find form.

Luke Oxley uses a mass of material which may or may not carry promise and meaning. Only a neon sign Books, Mags, Videos surrounded by the raw material of its own subject rings clear, full of pornographic and/or literary promise. This installation obscures content with form and hints at the desire of all artists to be disseminated through these media.

Square Head, Pale Face is a pastiche of early anthropological film. Francis Summers explores themes raised by the problematic photography of Edward Curtis who documented North American Indians at the beginning of this century; he manufactured the myth of the Indian image bringing props with him to alter the reality he found. To deal with this issue, Summers acts as both the observer and the observed, acting as the Indian and as Curtis.

Peter Richard's huge, unique pinhole photograph is a back to front record of the history of performance art. Within it, quite separately, groups or individuals act out or re-enact a distillation of moments. The artist engaged with live work, relates to the idea that art constantly needs to record itself. The work documents the continual frustration of performance artists in their bid to remain part of physical fact. The photograph itself defying permanence.

Jana Haldrich's performance carries the possibility of failure within the performance itself. She learns and recites a poem, each time apparently from the very start, and the process of her engagement is open to all. It exists somewhere between the process of a real time performance and the experience of a clear result.

Kenny Macleod's repetitive formula is annoying at first and then strangely compelling. At the beginning of every section, he introduces himself - Hello, my name is Robbie Fraser - but each time the story is different, revealing another layer of information, sometimes contradicting what we already know about him. It is seductive and sweet, using story-telling in a way that provides no stability. The narrative is real, or at least plausible, and its accumulation makes a kaleidoscope of truths, fictions and lies.

In Voices from Two Hemispheres, David Harding uses a magical film narrative to convey the inherent tension that exists between a schizophrenic individual, in his relation to the contemporary world and perhaps, more specifically to cultural identity. It is ambitious and fulsome. The narrative leads from claustrophobic study-room through cool and heightened fields of colour, flushes of external cultural reference and ends up with flourish of symbolism at the top of a mountain.

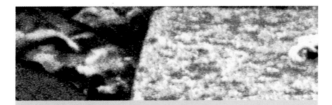

Charlie Birch sent out 49 postcards asking people to confess a sin for Scapegoat. This work uses the art gallery space as a sanctuary, where unpleasant secrets can be told. Just as in a confessional booth, the sins of the 49 participants in the work are not available to the public except by implication. The final collaged picture, with its dark association of religious imagery documents the collaborative process.

Cows breathe heavily in a field, sun drowns a courtyard, an open car drives into the city, facetious young girls joke about older men, a young woman meets her father on her birthday; in the series of short films by Louise Camrass. They are awkward and yet funny. Camrass manages in even more short time to convey the filmic equivalent of a short story.

Maddle Farm. It may be problematic to see such apparently simple representations of a landscape. Why should a bend in the road, angle of hedge and ploughed field extending across the horizon have any hold in contemporary vision? It gains attention because the associative romanticism of the rural, or artificial composition of directed gaze is denied by Louise Spence in these directly autonymous works.

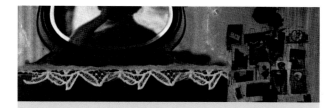

The prostitutes in a series of photographs from the beginning of the century have been removed from the picture. By digitally manipulating the archive subject Tim Meara opens up space which still, nonetheless, remains poignant. The work encourages an inevitable projection backwards in time onto early photography with its particular relation to documentation and art.

Some of the selected artists have submitted statements, either for the selection process or subsequently.

For her contribution, Carolyn Christov-Bakargiev has requested their inclusion in this catalogue.

The artist statements on the following spread have been selected and edited by Carolyn Christov- Bakargiev.

Athanasios Argianas I'm interested in mimicking, simulating already existing structures, more or less based on random processing, or, just a materiality which implies chance. Reflections, liquid formations, points, a clumsy trompe l'oeil are all elements hunting towards a 'compossible worlds' type of reality. I think these pieces have a dialogue with the reality of the representation and the reality of the process-object, a literal one. I'm interested in that distance between types of realism, as a kind of tautology and the absurd rationality of such a process. Or, it could all be some kind of special effects rejects, like a stunt-bag, which would be just as fine • **David Blandy** The virtual space is as shallow as the layer of pixels floating across the screen, a space that can only be experienced by two of the five senses. There is no life in this wood, this ring of trees, no unexpected glimpse of wildlife, no bird song. The viewer is suspended, caught in an endless loop, waiting for something to happen. In Ring, I have appropriated the backdrop of a computer game's fighting arena and removed all signifiers of its origin • **Cleo Broda** No map can tell you more than the person who made it wants you to know. I feel that all maps are subjective and it is this subjectivity which I intend to push and explore. The Local Information Guide will reveal what is behind the scenes of a particular place. It will show the traces of the inhabitants and offer information which is not usually surveyed and overtly converted. • **K.R Buxey** Legion is a slow and silent monochrome video installation, which re-configures footage of ecstatic women at music concerts in the late 1960's, in the light of contemporary ideas about language, vision and sexuality. I aim to articulate, through visual and spatial means, a particular position with regard to political and psychoanalytic discourse. I am committed to making heard particular voices and narratives, or, in drawing attention to their silence and their absence • **Kentoro Chiba** I have been drawing these scrolls over the past seven years. It is a form of figurative expression, but I have been trying to draw what comes naturally to mind, in order to encourage a flow of subconscious images. I don't have any particular idea in mind before forming these images. The direction of drawing is left to right, the opposite of traditional Japanese scrolls. Sometimes, I feel as if I were back in the past. There are two reasons why I named my work the Life Scroll. The first is the decision to continue drawing throughout my lifetime. The second is the intention to represent life as being linked, where creation and extinction both exist in an endless cycle.In the scroll, I often have to face some contradictions, when I employ techniques which were developed in Europe, such as perspective and the shade technique. Perspective, which can be considered as the expression of the moment is completely different from the scroll format, which represents the progression of time. These conflicts, however, seem to cause both unexpected and interesting results. For example, when I depict sunlight converging on a vanishing point, shadows form in parallel, horizontally, as they move away from the focus. The only way these results can be avoided is by increasing the number of vanishing points on the horizon. It is illogical that there can be over three focal points on the horizon, at the same time. It proves that perspective is a view from one fixed point, and works only when the picture is cut out from a small piece of the world, in the sense of both time and space. I believe that the scroll started to exist when I put pen to paper. Often, I have feelings that the scroll forces me to draw on it. So, it might be a natural result that time and space became an important theme of mine, because I have been keen to watch what is going on in my art. Thus, my attitude toward art is more similar to that of an observer rather than that of an artist • **Ben Cook** The Found Paintings are reappropriated fabrics which were originally destined for the manufacture of football shirts. They were flawed during production in a printed textiles factory and the artist has represented them as abstract paintings, by placing them on to stretchers and applying the visual language of abstract painting. The Found Painting series developed out of a process of culling material from his immediate environment (that of the last vestiges of Manchester's textile-based industry) and interrogating and arranging it using the visual vocabulary learnt from a singular painting practice. The flawed/faulted fabrics, or computer generated designs for fabrics are the product of manufacturing mistakes in production • **Richard Cuerden** Having trained as a classical dancer, moving into commercial theatre to performing in musicals such as 42nd Street, Cats and Chess, I experienced a lifetime of performance • **Layla Curtis** The United Kingdom is a carefully manipulated map of the UK, where the Kingdoms of England and Scotland are presented as separate islands. It is not coincidental to the piece that the location in which I created this work was Edinburgh,

Capital of a devolving Scotland. I am aware of the influence this particular location has had on the work • **Clare Gasson** This piece drawn in red lipstick, suggests a void, a fissure, an orifice, a psychological opening - a mental space. Within its form the line also questions the framework of architectural and ideological space • **David Harding** Voices from Two Hemispheres. How should we live? How should we exist? The film journeys from a left-brained way of living, its associated values and cultural hemisphere, through the central divide (transformation through cinema?) onto a spiritual quest in the right-brain hemisphere, to find a different way of thinking, of living and different values. Many psychological references are used - thresholds (going through holes, doorways, crossing bridges), directions, signs and climbing, split images and reflection, shining lights as connections, ruins as memory, blocking out colour, cinema as transition and as transfiguring, photographs as dead object, music as mood and, cultural reference and disturbance, sectional contrast with location and contents, with lighting (light, dark, colour), with camera and editing styles, and hybrid contrast within and across readings • **Ian Kiaer** I'm using fragmentary motifs to reflect on biblical subjects. In this case Deuteronomy 11:29 (Dt. 27,28). The model form seems to offer the informal possibility of looking on -theatrium mundi. A means of play • **Stefanie Marshall** My work is organically multidisciplinary • **Tim Meara** My current work, culminating in the Storyville series stems from a re-analysis of a photographic archive. In 1912, E.J. Bellocq made a collection of photographs of the prostitutes of Storyville in New Orleans. These are the only photographs he is known to have taken. My work involves digitally removing the subjects from these images, leaving small traces of their presence. The work uses associations of the original series, but focuses on the space around the subject, emphasising the relationship of the male gaze to female subject. My work plays on this fascination with the photograph as the frozen moment, manipulated and never real, always appearing as a fetish • **Katie Pratt** Paint is irreverently encouraged to drip, buckle and wrinkle, posing a moment where control could slip away. But, by formulaically highlighting the creases and imperfections in the paint, events are reclaimed and converted to my own unashamedly-literal language. • **D.J Simpson.** The normal logic of figure and ground are reversed in these negative reliefs. The scale of the larger paintings affords the work a lavish scrutiny that avoids the strictures of the DIY enthusiast • **Louise Spence** This project considers the crisis of identity, doubt and uncertainty facing rural Britain, the land and those who live on it • **Francis Summers** This work was made with three themes in mind: the impossibility of the neutral image; the non-existence of the stable subject and the appropriation of history by dominant political and economic forces. I set the work in the context of the anthropological documentation of the North American Indian, which coincided with the invention of cinema and the Hollywood narrative. The work deals mainly with themes raised by the problematic photography of Edward Curtis. I felt that in staging the piece in the supposedly primal sphere of the wilderness, whilst refuting the possibility of such a stable and masculine position, this problem of a male attempt at claiming the ground of identity politics could be articulated. With the use of the square mask, devoid of features, upon which any reading can be projected and deflected, I felt I was attempting to articulate the enlightenment project's attempt to organise and formulate set modes of identity. My solution was to articulate the visual fact that identity is neither set, nor is it possible to describe. Not objectifying another subject felt in some ways logically impossible. So, I set out to objectify my self and examine the possible modes of identity that could be both created and found there. In short, I set out to both frame certain problems and situate my self within this field. Framing and being framed, as the saying goes • **Julian Walker** My original intention in making works of this kind was to use the act of collecting to fill the vision, to make work that would act like a Rothko painting, to give the viewer an experience that would visually echo the obsessions of collecting, and enable engagement with the different ways of seeing the objects from different viewpoints • **Nicole Wermers** I work with video as a way of reclaiming space, using editing as a way of constructing potential endless buildings. Palisades shows an upside-down camera ride and gives the impression of somebody walking on the ceilings of various rooms, exploring virgin territory and quite literally referring to Michel de Certeaus description of walking as a way of making space (The Art of Doing). By the change of perspective, I am appropriating space which wasn't previously available and to me appears very desirable.

Athanasios Argianas

B.1976 Athens, Greece
1999 Kunstakademie Dusseldorf, Klasse Prof. Jannis Kounellis
1998-99 PG Dip. Fine Art, Byam Shaw School of Art, London
1997-98 visiting student PGCE Fine Art, Goldsmiths College, University of London
1994-97 BA School of Fine Art, Aristotle University, Thessaloniki

RECENT EXHIBITIONS
1999 Halfway to Highgate, Lauderdale House in collaboration with Kingsgate Gallery, London
1997 15 & 15 site work in collaboration with Kunstakademie Dusseldorf Warehouse 1 & Yeni Tzami, Thessaloniki
Vice Versa, Paratiritis Gallery, Thessaloniki

Charlie Birch

B.1977 Hastings, England
1997-99 BA Critical Fine Art Practice, Central St Martins School of Art and Design, London
1996-97 Foundation in Art and Design, Chelsea College of Art, London

RECENT EXHIBITIONS
1999 Art in Time Festival, University of Wales Institute, Cardiff
1998 Cohen Woolfe Prize, Lethaby Gallery, Central St Martins
1998 Merge, Byam Shaw School of Art

Charlie Birch was brought up in Portugal and now lives and works in London. Much of her work explores the areas of myth and fairy tales, religion and iconography. Her practice is based in photography as well as video and performance.

David Blandy

B.1976 London
1995-98 BA Fine Art Sculpture, Chelsea College of Art, London
1994-95 Foundation, Chelsea College of Art

RECENT EXHIBITIONS
1999 Medway Open, Gillingham, Kent
1998 Originals 2, Kapil Jariwala Gallery, London
1997 Virtual Burial Ground, Moravian Burial Ground, Chelsea, London
1997 Minus 4, Fridge Gallery, Brixton, London

Cleo Broda

B.1970 Edinburgh
1996-98 MFA Print, Slade School of Fine Art, University College London
1989-93 BA Fine Art Painting, Glasgow School of Art
1988-89 Freshman Foundation, Rhode Island School of Design

RECENT EXHIBITIONS
1998 Mislaid, Slade Radio Live Internet Radio Broadcast, ICA bar event, London
1998 MAP, Crowbar Coffee, London
1998 Good News from the Vatican, Fishe, London
1997 Macumenta, Tramway, Glasgow
1997 Test Site 2, Gallery A, London
1996 Their Chromakey and Ours, Waygood, Newcastle upon Tyne

K. R Buxey

B.1967 Reading, England
1999 MFA Goldsmiths College, University of London
1996-99 BA Critical Fine Art Practice, University of Brighton
1995-96 Foundation, North Oxfordshire College of Art

RECENT EXHIBITIONS
1999 Legion, David Stainer Memorial Space, University of Brighton
1998 Undergraduate Show, Hopkins Hall, Ohio State University, Columbus, Ohio
1997 It's A Girl, David Stainer Memorial Space, University of Brighton

Louise Camrass

B.1969 London
1997-99 MFA Royal College of Art, London
1989-94 BA Fine Art, Central St Martins School of Art and Design, London

RECENT EXHIBITIONS
1998 Film and Video Festivals in Helsinki, Leeds, Maidstone, London, San Francisco
1997 Ritzy Cinema London, Glastonbury Festival, Perth Film Festival Scotland

Kentaro Chiba

B.1953 Tokyo, Japan
1998-99 visiting Student MFA, Central St Martins School of Art and Design, London
1997-98 MFA, Nottingham Trent University
1973-78 BA Fine Art, Yokohama National University, Japan

RECENT EXHIBITIONS
1999 Central St Martins School of Art and Design
1998 International Print Triennial, Kanagawa, Japan
1998 Group show of MA students from St Martins, Poland Street, London,
1998 The Bonington Gallery Foyer, Nottingham
1996 Ono Gallery, Tokyo
1996 Takaoka City Museum Gallery, Takaoka Toyama Prefecture

AWARDS
1994 Osaka Triennial Special Prize
1992 Artex 92 Golden Prize

Ben Cook

B.1967 Gloucestershire, England
1997-98 MA Painting, Manchester Metropolitan University
1986-89 BA Painting, University of Sunderland

Ben Cook has held several solo exhibitions and has been included in many group shows, most notably John Moores 18, Walker Art Gallery Liverpool 1993 and East, Norwich in the same year. The series of Found Paintings won the 1998 Pebeo International Painting competition in Marseilles France. Ben Cook's work is held in the collections of Whitworth Art Gallery Manchester, Atlas Manchester and the Arts Council of England.

Richard Cuerden

B.1963 Walton-le-Dale, England
1999 MA Painting Royal College of Art, London
1996-99 BA Fine Art, Winchester School of Art

RECENT EXHIBITIONS
1998 New Artists 98, John Martin Gallery, London
1997 Recent Paintings, Sutton House The National Trust, London
1996 Commission for a series of paintings for the opening of the Cameron Mackintosh musical Martin Guerre, London
1996 Art 96, Business Design Centre, London

Andrew Currie

B.1977 Dolgellau, Wales
1996-99 BA Fine Art, Falmouth College of Arts

RECENT EXHIBITIONS
1999 Big Warm Open, Cambridge Darkroom, Cambridge
1999 Breaks and Pieces, Stanley Picker Gallery, Kingston
1999 6 Art Colleges, RWA, Bristol

AWARDS
1998 Denis Mitchell Sculpture Prize

Layla Curtis

B.1975 Chippenham, England
1999 MA Sculpture, Chelsea College of Art, London
1997 L'Ecole des Artes Decoratifs, Strasbourg, France, Exchange Programme
1994-98 BA Painting, Edinburgh College of Art
1993-94 Foundation, University of Sunderland

RECENT EXHIBITIONS
1999 Mapping, Akiyoshidai International Arts Village, Japan
1999 For a Totally Absorbing Time, Idei, Himeji, Japan
1998 ECA at the Royal Bank of Scotland, Edinburgh International Festival
1998 Royal Scottish Academy Annual Exhibition

AWARDS
1998 Helen Rose Bequest for Distinguished work
1998 Andrew Guest Bequest Scholarship, First Prize

After graduating, Layla lived in Japan for one year. She took part in a residency programme at Akiyoshidai International Arts Village where she developed her hybrid maps series and held her first solo show. Following the residency she stayed in Japan and organised a group show of young artists living in Himeji and worked with students at Himeji Shikisai High School.
An Andrew Guest Bequest Scholarship enabled a trip to Belize, Central America where she worked as a volunteer in 1998. While travelling in Europe in May 1997, Layla organised a one month project, involving 14 participants across 9 countries in 14 Simultaneous Walks in Europe.

Jane Fox

B.1958 New Tredegar ,South Wales
1999 MA Fine Art Sculpture, Royal College of Art, London
1995-99 BA Fine Art, Slade School of Fine Art, University College London
1991 St Davids Hospital Bangor, Welsh National Board Teaching Certificate
1986 University Hospital Wales, Registered Health Visitor
1982-85 BSc Psychology, University College Cardiff
1981 University Hospital Wales, Registered Midwife
1979 University Hospital Wales, State Registered Nurse

RECENT EXHIBITIONS
1998 Highgate Cemetary Performance Collaboration with photographer Jessica Robinson
1996 The Big Issue, Group Show London
1995 Bloomsbury Theatre Performance Collaboration with Kate Freeland and Foyer exhibition of Drawings

AWARDS
1998/97 Slade Bursary
1997 The Prankard Jones Memorial Prize
1996 The Monnington Prize
1996 South Square Bursary, University College London

Clare Gasson

B. Birmingham
1996-99 BA Fine Art, Goldsmiths College, University of London
1994-96 Foundation, Sir John Cass School of Art, London Guildhall

RECENT EXHIBITIONS
1999 Bankside Browser, Tate Gallery of Modern Art at St Christopher House, London

Jana Haldrich

B. 1974 Apolda, Germany
1999 MA Fine Art, Royal College of Art, London
1997-99 BA Fine Art, Chelsea College of Art and Design, London
1996-97 BTEC Foundation, Kingsway College

RECENT EXHIBITIONS
1999 X-hibit, LISU, London
1999 Freshly Dawn, LWHS, London
1998 Extremities, Moravian Burial Ground, Chelsea, London
1998 Below Zero, Trinity Buoy Wharf, London
1998 Spill the Beans, Joceline Andrews, London
1998 Stable, TMW, London

David Harding

David Harding has worked with tribal peoples in South India, with craftworkers in Colombia, and has travelled through 50 countries. His filmwork celebrates different cultures and different ways of living, challenging western values. Working for Third World development, he continues to travel, write, photograph and make films.

RECENT EXHIBITIONS
1999 7th Festival Chileno, Internacional del Cortometraje, Santiago, Chile
1999 39th International Film Festival for Children and Youth, Zlin, Czech Republic
1999 14th Videoformes, Clermont-Ferrand, France
1998 15th Video-Film-Tagen, Thuringen & Rheinland-Pfalz, Germany
1998 26th Festival der Nationen, Ebensee, Austria
1999 38th International Film Festival for Children and Youth
1998 Long Shots, 1st International Student Film Festival, Glasgow University
1997 2nd European Student Film Festival, London

Julie Henry

B. 1959 Cambridge, England
1993-98 BA Critical Fine Art Practice, Central St Martins School of Art and Design, London
1992-93 Foundation, Mornington Centre, London
1990-92 HND Theatre Costume, London College of Fashion
1989-90 BTEC Theatre Design, North Herts College

RECENT EXHIBITIONS
1999 World Cup 98: The Final, London Printworks Trust, Brixton
1998 Going Down, Croydon Clock Tower, London
1998 Volcano Festival, Oval House, London
1997 My Eyes My Eyes, The Silo, Greenwich and Milch Gallery, London
1997 Zone, Multi-media Arts Festival, Maidstone, Kent
1997 Six British Artists, Ars Locus Gallery, Tokyo, Japan
In collaboration with Debbie Bragg.

Ian Kiaer

B. 1971 London
1998 MA Painting, Royal College of Art, London
1991-95 BA Fine Art, Slade School of Fine Art, University College London
1990-91 Foundation, Wimbledon School of Art, London

RECENT EXHIBITIONS
1995 Memory, Riverside Studios, London

AWARDS
1998 The Basil H. Alkazzi Foundation Scholarship Award
1995 The Duveen Travel Scholarship Award

Natasha Kidd

B. 1973 Ontario, Canada

Natasha Kidd completed her foundation course at West Cheshire College in 1991 entering the Slade School of Fine Art in the same year. In 1993, she organised and exhibited in Detour, a group show at a disused bus depot behind Kings Cross Station. In 1996, she graduated from the Slade and then entered their postgraduate school the following year. She completed her MFA in painting in 1998.

Natasha Kidd has since shown in Broadcast, a group exhibition at the Kingsgate Gallery in London. She has taught at Winchester and Chelsea College of Art and is currently part of the education team at the Chisenhale Gallery, where she has developed projects for students with Special Education Needs.

Nick Laessing

B. 1973 London
1996-99 Sculpture, Royal Academy Schools, London
1993-96 Intermedia, Kingston University
1995 Dusseldorf Art Academy, Exchange Programme

RECENT EXHIBITIONS
1998 It Happens Everyday 2, W139 Gallery, Amsterdam
1998 I was an infinitely hot and dense dot, The Stanley Picker Gallery, Kingston upon Thames
1997 Advent, R. Newbold Gallery, Covent Garden, London
1996 It Happens Everyday 1, 137 Chatsworth Road, London
1996 Dusseldorf Kunst Akademie Rundgang, Germany

AWARDS
1998 British Institute Award
1998 Henry Moore Project Fund
1998 Ray Finnis Charitable Trust Award
1997 Royal Academy Landseer Scholarship
1997 Marantz Electronics Sponsorship

Kenny Macleod

B. 1967	Aberdeen
2000-02	Rijksakademie van Beeldende Kunsten, Amsterdam
1996-99	BA Fine Art, Goldsmiths College, University of London
1995-96	Foundation, The City Lit, London
1985-90	MA French/Philosophy, University of Edinburgh

RECENT EXHIBITIONS

| 1999 | SYZYGY O(rphan) d(rift>) Event, Beaconsfield, London |

AWARDS

| 1998 | Hamad Butt Fine Art Award, Goldsmiths College |

Stefanie Marshall

B. 1967	Ontario, Canada
1999	MA Fine Arts Performance and Installation, Bretton Hall, University of Leeds
1995	AOCA, Ontario College of Art
1993	BA Fine Art, York University, Toronto, Ontario

RECENT EXHIBITIONS

1997	Dolls Reclaimed, Ontario Craft Gallery, Toronto
1997	Medium 4, International Exhibition of Living Art Documentation, St Gheorghe Art Gallery, Romania
1997	12th Performance Art Festival, Forest City Gallery, London, Ontario
1997	10th Cleveland Performance Art Festival, Cleveland, Ohio
1997	7A*11D Performance Art Festival, Toronto
1996	9th Cleveland Performance Art Festival, Cleveland, Ohio
1995	In Too Out Of, Gallery Gong, Toronto

AWARDS

| 1994-97 | O.A.C. Exhibition Assistance Grant |
| 1993 | Fine Arts Merit Award |

Tim Meara

B. 1977	Reading, England
1996-99	BA Fine Art, Sheffield Hallam University
1995-96	Foundation, Amersham and Wycombe College

RECENT EXHIBITIONS

1999	There's no Sexual Relation, Centre For Freudian Research, London
1998	The Physiognomy of Insanity, Sheffield Hallam University
1998	Print Unlimited, Psalter Lane Gallery, Sheffield

Nathaniel Mellors

B. 1974	Doncaster, England
1999	MA Sculpture, Royal College of Art, London
1996-99	BA Fine Art, Ruskin School of Drawing and Fine Art, Oxford

RECENT EXHIBITIONS

1998	Platato's Hypothetical Productions, New College Oxford
1998	Hermes Love Bug, Bullingdon Road Studios, Oxford
1998	The Wall Medley, Ruskin School, Oxford
1998	Sometimes Love Just Ain't Enough, The Custard Factory, Birmingham
1998	Sehenswurdigkeiten, Quedlinburg, Germany
1997	Mellors 27.10.97 - 31.10.97, Dolphin Gallery, Oxford

AWARDS

| 1998 | Mitzi Cunliffe Sculpture Prize |

Luke Oxley

B. 1968	Folkestone, England
1999	MA Fine Art, Goldsmiths College, University of London
1988-91	BA Sculpture, West Surrey Institute of Art and Design

RECENT EXHIBITIONS

1999	Non Stop Opening, Central Point Gallery, London
1999	Museum of Me, The Museum of....., London
1999	Product Placement, The Levi's Gallery, London
1998	Object Pornography, The Banqueting House, London

Katie Pratt

B. 1969	Epsom, England
1996-98	MA Painting, Royal College of Art, London
1989-92	BA Fine Art, Winchester School of Art
1987-88	Foundation, Central School of Art and Design

RECENT EXHIBITIONS

1999	Painting and Time, The Nunnery, London
1999	Don't Smoke in My House, Cremer, London
1998	Original 2, Kapil Jariwala Gallery, London
1996	TPI Gallery, Surrey
1996	Southwark Open, South London Gallery
1996	London Group Biennale, Barbican Art Gallery, London
1995	Artist for the Day, Flowers East, London
1992-93	Germinations, touring Grenoble, Budapest, Bratislawa

AWARDS

1998	Daler Rowney Painting Award
1997	Socrates Award, Berlin
1997	John Crane Award, New York

Peter Richards

B. 1970 Cardiff, Wales
1999 M.Phil Fine Art, University of Ulster at Belfast
1996 PGD Fine Art, University of Ulster at Belfast
1995 PGC Fine Art, University of Ulster at Belfast
1994 BA Fine Art, University of Wales, Cardiff

RECENT EXHIBITIONS
1999 Another Something Other, The Golden Thread Gallery, Belfast
1999 Through a Glass Darkly, Het Consortium, Amsterdam
1998 The National Review of Live Art, The Arches, Glasgow
1998 Camera Lucida, The Old Museum Arts Centre, Belfast
1998 Performance Lucida, The Context Gallery, Derry
1998 Ashowabouttime, Milch Gallery, London
1998 Photo 98, Hull Time Based Arts
1998 Infusion 98, Real Art Project, Limerick
1998 Fix 98, Belfast
1998 NI gulP, Plug In Gallery, Winnipeg
1998 Art from Belfast, Idaho Gallery, Chicago
1998 Still to Real, Transmission, Glasgow
1998 Reverend Todds Full House, Grassy Knoll Productions, Belfast
1997 L'Evenement Oblique, Tangente, Montreal
1997 European Couples and Others, Transmission Gallery, Glasgow

Gaylie Runciman

B. 1961 Glasgow
1995-98 BA Fine Art Sculpture, Glasgow School of Art

RECENT EXHIBITIONS
1998 Lapland, British Council, Edinburgh
1998 Streetworks, Street Level, King St, Glasgow
1998 Let's Play Risk, Juice, Earlham St, London
1998 Lapland Christmas Show, Glasgow

D.J Simpson

B. 1966 Lancaster
1996-98 MA Fine Art, Goldsmiths College, University of London
1986-90 BA Fine Art, Reading University

RECENT EXHIBITIONS
1999 Solo show, Site, Dusseldorf
1999 Solo show, Morrison Judd Gallery, London
1999 Heart and Soul, 60 Long Lane, London
1999 Group show, Galerie Hollenbach, Stuttgart
1999 Formerly, Jerwood Gallery, London
1999 Elastic Abstract, Curtain Road Arts, London
1999 Ways of Living, RMIT Project Space, Victoria, Australia
1998 Underbelly, Cosmopolitan Cinema, Adelaide, Australia
1998 Cluster Bomb, Morrison Judd Gallery, London
1998 Group Show, Galerie Y- Burg, Amsterdam
1998 Ultra Gnost, Sali Gia Gallery, London
1998 Grupp Show, Proposition Gallery, Belfast
1998 One Night Pub, Unit, London
1998 Underworld, Australian Studios, London
1998 Party 1998, KSS, London

Louise Spence

B. 1965 Berkshire, England
1996-99 BA Photography, London College of Printing
1995-96 BTECH National Diploma Art and Design, Kensington and Chelsea College, London

Jayne Stokes

B. 1973 Shropshire, England
1997-98 MA Fine Art, Winchester School of Art
1997 Exchange Programme Barcelona
1992-96 BA Drawing and Painting, Edinburgh College of Art
1991-92 National Diploma Art and Design, Shrewsbury College of Art and Technology

RECENT EXHIBITIONS
1999 12month residency based in Buckinghamshire, supported by Southern Arts, Buckinghamshire and Chiltern University College and the Arts Education Forum
1999 Platform, The Old Billiard Room, Platform 3, Peckham Rye Train Station, London
1999 Uncommon Objects, Wandsworth Museum, London
1999 Bankside Browser, Tate Gallery of Modern Art at St Christopher House, London
1998 Inhabit, The Panorama Space, Barro de Ferro, Barcelona
1998 Unearthed, Grizedale Forest Gallery, Cumbria
1998 Viewpoints, Artsway Open Exhibition, New Forest, Hampshire
1998 Intervencions, site-specific work, Barcelona
1997 2 month residency at Grizedale Sculpture Forest, Cumbria

Francis Summers

B. 1975 Strathroy, Canada
1998-99 MA History of Art, Courtauld Institute of Art, London
1995-98 BA Fine Art, Wimbledon School of Art, London
1994-95 Foundation, Wimbledon School of Art, London

RECENT EXHIBITIONS
1998 Cold Front, Bricks and Kicks Gallery, Vienna
1997 Out, curated by Richard Wentworth, Wimbledon Library, London
1996 Back to the Future, National Gallery, London
1995 Live Art, Byam Shaw School of Art, London

Julian Walker

1954 London
1999 PHD Fine Art, University of East
London
91-92 PG Fine Art, Central St Martins
School of Art and Design,
London
86-91 Diploma Art and Design, Sir John
Cass School of Art, City of
London Polytechnic
73-77 MA English Literature,
St Andrews University

RECENT EXHIBITIONS
1998 Worcester Collected, Worcester
City Museum and Art Gallery
1998 Mr & Mrs Walker Have Moved,
Kettle's Yard, Cambridge
1998 Souvenirs, Museum Street,
London
1997 Residency at Natural History
Museum, London
1997 The Magpie Instinct, Booth
Museum of Natural History,
Brighton
1996 The International Occasional
Museum of Collecting,
International Collecting
Conference, Leicester University
1996 Evidence, IKON Gallery touring,
Birmingham
1996 Terms of Exchange, VisionFest,
Liverpool

Nicole Wermers

1969 Emsdetten, Germany
1999 MA Fine Art, Central St Martins
School of Art and Design, London
990-97 Hochschule fur Bildende Kunst,
Hamburg, Germany

RECENT EXHIBITIONS
1999 Young German Artists in Britain,
Goethe Institute, London
1998 Osygus, Produzenten Galerie
Hamburg
1998 Echopark, Bieber-Haus, Hamburg
1998 Laden, Gunther Resky,
Schillerstrasse, Berlin
1997 Diplomandenausstellung, K3,
Hamburg

AWARDS
998-99 DAAD Jahresstipendium London
1997 Award of the Dietze Foundation,
Hamburg

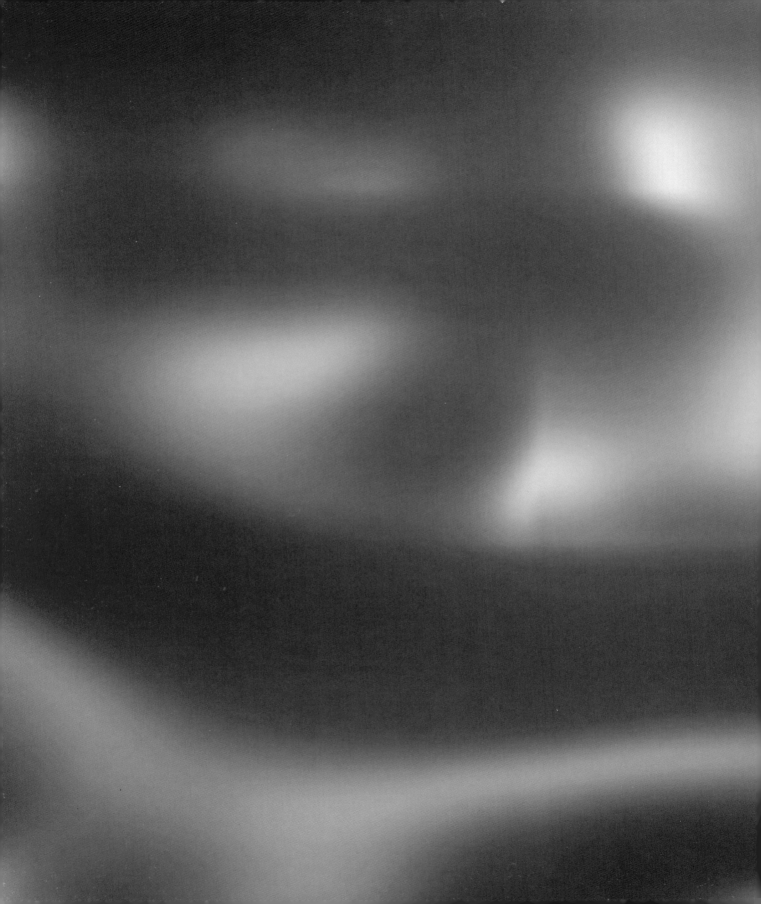

Acknowledgements

New Contemporaries 99 is launched in Liverpool as an integral part of the first Liverpool Biennial of Contemporary Art. The move to initiate a UK based Biennial, in the city of Liverpool, to rival the scale and ambition of some of the established Biennale's world wide, is brave and visionary. We are delighted to be part of the adventure.

This is the third year we will have launched the exhibition in Liverpool. The Board of Directors of New Contemporaries are grateful to the Trustees of the Nigel Moores Family Charitable Foundation for their continuing support of the exhibition and the opportunities they bring in the connection with the city of Liverpool.

New Contemporaries 99 is very much the product of teamwork. Organisationally, we have benefited from the embrace of the Liverpool Biennial, which has helped to support us in terms of venue development, marketing and education. I would like to thank Elizabeth-anne Williams, for her incredible energy and zeal and all the Biennial team.

We exist, as an organisation, to provide new and emerging artists, trained in the UK with an opportunity to be seen and flourish. This year, New Contemporaries 99 will be shown alongside Trace, the international exhibition curated by Anthony Bond for The Liverpool Biennial, in the Exchange Flags venue. This presents a unique opportunity for the work of a new generation of artists to be seen alongside their international peer group.

The ground floor of Exchange Flags has been specially-converted to temporarily house the two exhibitions; providing a beautiful and expansive space. As ever, the achievement of Exchange Flags is the result of the energy and commitment of an extensive team of individuals against a back-drop of limited resources and a race against time. We should recognise the hard work behind-the-scenes- to enable these spaces. We would especially like to thank Cindy Hubert, Project Manager for the Biennial and the technical crew headed by Gary Dyson: Steve Connah, Rob Carr, John Smith, Dean Woolford, John Murray, Lee Dyson. Each year, the show challenges our technological knowledge and resources, and we are grateful to Tom Cullen for his technical expertise and problem-solving.

New Contemporaries 99 at Exchange Flags is funded by North West Arts Board and the Foundation for sport and the arts.

New Contemporaries 99 will again tour to London, but ambitiously across a three venue collaboration of South London spaces: South London Gallery, Milch and Beaconsfield. Thinking through how the show might work across three independent spaces has been invigorating and exciting. We welcome the participation of David Thorp and Donna Lynas at South London Gallery, Lisa Painting and Fred Mann at Milch, Naomi Siderfin and David Crawforth at Beaconsfield. The South London Collaboration is supported by the London Arts Board.

The production of this year's show has been especially adventurous and I would personally like to thank all the artists for their commitment to the project; Robin Klassnik, Des Lawrence and Sacha Craddock who give so freely of their time as Board members and Simon Morrissey who is helping to co-ordinate the South London collaboration.

1999 has seen the development of a new turn in the relationship with the Arts Council of England, which we hope will lead us to a more stable and sustainable future. We are grateful to both Eileen Daly and Jeremy Theophilus for their support.

Finally, I would like to thank James Moores. This year has seen a huge demand on his time and a far greater level of personal commitment. We look forward to the part we can play in the founding of the Liverpool Biennial of Contemporary Art as a signature event, and the promise it holds for the cultural mapping of Liverpool. We are pleased to be associated not least, for the assertion it holds for an optimistic future for artists and the visual arts.

Bev Bytheway

with the support of the Nigel Moores Family Charitable
Foundation

catalogue

edited by Bev Bytheway
design by Alan Ward, assisted by Dominic Legge @ Axis
printed by Record Print, Manchester
reprographics by Leeds Photo Litho
images supplied by the artist unless stated otherwise
inside cover photography by Matt Squire,
views from roof of Walker House, Exchange Flags,
Liverpool

artists acknowlegements:
Natasha Kidd thanks Crown Paint for their support
Clare Gasson's Lipstick Line is sponsored by Bourjois

@ New Contemporaries (1988) Ltd and the artists
Published by New Contemporaries (1988) Ltd

ISBN 0 9515556 8 5